CHARLES DICKENS

and the making of

A CHRISTMAS CAROL

D1715109

CHARLES DICKENS

and the making of

A CHRISTMAS CAROL

by

Michael Norris

2011
New Street Communications, LLC
Wickford, RI

newstreetcommunications.com

Published 2011

New Street Communications, LLC
Wickford, Rhode Island
newstreetcommunications.com

Cover illustration: Portrait of Charles Dickens circa 1860 by Alexander
Glasgow.

New Street Development Editor
William Renehan

CONTENTS

The young Charles Dickens drawn by his friend Daniel Maclise in 1839, four years before A Christmas Carol.

I

A National Benefit

When Charles Dickens's *A Christmas Carol* appeared on December 19th, 1843, critics and readers alike hailed it immediately as a classic. For many in Victorian England, the *Carol* represented much more than mere entertainment; it was viewed, rather, as a summons to the true Christian spirit of generosity and tolerance in all men and women. The first printing of 6000 copies sold out on the first day of publication. *A Christmas Carol* went through five additional printings before Christmas day, with some 15,000 sold by the New Year at five shillings apiece - a quite modest price.

The literary magazine of the London Athenaeum described Dickens's ghostly story as "a tale to make the reader laugh and cry - to open his hands, and open his heart to charity even toward the uncharitable ... a dainty dish to set before a King." Poet and editor Thomas Hood raved: "If Christmas, with its ancient and hospitable customs, its social and charitable observances, were ever in danger of decay, this is the book that would give them a new lease. The very name of the author predisposes one to the kindlier feelings; and a peep at the Frontispiece sets the animal spirits capering ... ."

Writing in *Fraser's Magazine*, William Makepeace Thackeray declared the *Carol* "a national benefit and to every man or woman who reads it, a personal kindness. The last two people I heard speak of it were women; neither knew the other, or the author, and both said, by way of criticism, 'God bless him!'" Speaking of the character Tiny Tim, Thackeray wrote: "There is not a reader in England but that little creature will be a bond of union between the author and him; and he will say of Charles Dickens, as the woman just now, 'GOD BLESS HIM!' What a feeling this is for a writer to inspire, and what a reward to reap!"

Even the critic Theodore Martin, who normally despised Dickens's sentimentality and sensationalism, spoke glowingly of the *Carol*. Martin described the story as "finely felt, and calculated to work much social good." Dickens himself noted that he received "by every post, all manner of strangers writing all manner of letters about their homes and hearths, and how the *Carol* is read aloud there, and kept on a very little shelf by itself."

Lord Francis Jeffrey - critic and former editor of the *Edinburgh Review* for whom, a few weeks later, Dickens would name a son - was perhaps the most strident of the *Carol's* fans. Addressing Dickens personally, Jeffrey told the author he should be happy "for you may be sure you have done more good by this little publication, fostered more kindly feelings, and prompted more positive acts of beneficence, than can be traced to all the pulpits of Christendom since Christmas, 1842."

Dickens's younger contemporary, the Scottish novelist Margaret Oliphant, deplored what she described as the quaint "plum pudding" aspects of the book. Nevertheless, she acknowledged that in the days of its first publication the *Carol* was regarded as "a new gospel," - a work of literature unique in that it actually made people behave better after reading it.

Two months following the *Carol's* initial publication, in reviewing a recently opened dramatic adaptation (first among hundreds), the theater critic for *The Illustrated London News* commented: "When a late celebrated scholar and critic made the witty remark that Boz [Dickens] 'would go up like a rocket and come down like a stick,' he forgot in his prediction to say how long the rocket's brilliancy would endure! In our thinking the said rocket has taken root (if we may be allowed the expression) in the sky of intellect, and with its offshoots of light, every one of which becomes more luminous daily, we might say voluminous indeed, will, we have no doubt, be considered by future literary astronomers, a constellation! Dickens is a great man - a moral chymist [sic] who has analyzed the human heart to a nicety. 'Shewing the poison and the honey there.'"

Modern critic Alex Ogg notes that when *A Christmas Carol* was published in December 1843, Dickens was "already Britain's foremost writer, and increasingly active in social reform. At the time the author considered it 'his most prodigious success,' and the novel has never been out of print ... since. [The book has been] constantly reinvented and reinterpreted down the generations, powered by a moral core that is both unambiguous and timeless. Ebenezer Scrooge, the solitary, misanthropic miser, remains central to its enduring appeal, to the extent that his name is a more recognizable entity to audiences than the story itself."

Indeed, the *Carol* remains as vibrant with us today as it has ever been, infusing and influencing nearly every aspect of Christmas as celebrated across the western world. The book is read and reread by millions each year. Through the decades, beautifully wrought editions have been illustrated by the likes of Arthur Rackham, A.I. Keller, George Alfred Williams, Everett Shinn, and Harry Furniss, all working in the fine tradition of Dickens's original partner in the book, John Leech.

But even more people experience the *Carol* as performance. (This writer's first exposure to the work was as a six year old watching a televised cartoon version starring Mr. Magoo.) The ranks of film Scrooges include Alastair Sim, Basil Rathbone, Reginald Owen, Sir Ralph Richardson, Sir Laurence Olivier, Sir Alec Guinness, Ronald Coleman, Albert Finney, Bill Murray, George C. Scott, Jim Carrey, Patrick Stewart and Michael Caine (the latter in collaboration with the Muppets). Lionel Barrymore portrayed him annually on the radio from 1934 to 1953.

Hundreds of stage productions of the *Carol* are produced every year across the British Isles, North America and elsewhere. (The list of dramatists who have adapted the *Carol* includes George S. Kaufman and Maxwell Anderson.) The book has been scored for ballet more than once, most notably by Ralph Vaughan Williams. And there have even been operas, the most well known of which is Thea Musgrave's of 1979. Dickens's own legendary live readings

of the *Carol* have been frequently recreated, not the least
by Patrick Stewart, Roy Dotrice and the author's great-
great-grandson, actor Gerald Charles Dickens. As a
performance vehicle, the *Carol* ranks with *The Nutcracker*
as a staple of the Holidays.

Old Scrooge himself, meanwhile, has become a double-
sided emblem. On the one hand, his name is synonymous
with all the characteristics of the ultimate "economic man"
- miserliness, meanness, and every form of self-absorbed,
uncharitable behavior. "Don't be a Scrooge," we'll say - and
everyone immediately knows to whom and what we refer.
On the other hand, the old man has as well become a
symbol for the possibilities of redemption, reinvention and
second-chances. He is "saved" by the ghosts who, through
their visits, rekindle a vital fire in his cold heart. As the
story closes, generosity of spirit has been renewed within
Scrooge, and it is clear that a liberal kindness will
henceforth guide his actions. As Dickens wrote: "Scrooge
became as good a friend, as good a master, and as good a
man, as the good old city knew, or any other good old city,
town, or borough, in the good old world. Some people
laughed to see the alteration in him, but he let them laugh,
and little heeded them; for he was wise enough to know
that nothing ever happened on this globe, for good, at

which some people did not have their fill of laughter in the outset; and knowing that such as these would be blind anyway, he thought it quite as well that they should wrinkle up their eyes in grins, as have the malady in less attractive forms. His own heart laughed: and that was quite enough for him."

G. K. Chesterton called the *Carol* "a kind of philanthropic dream, an enjoyable nightmare, in which the scenes shift bewilderingly and seem as miscellaneous as the pictures in a scrap-book, but in which there is one constant state of the soul, a state of rowdy benediction and a hunger for human faces. The beginning is about a winter day and a miser; yet the beginning is in no way bleak. The author starts with a kind of happy howl; he bangs on our door like a drunken carol singer; his style is festive and popular; he compares the snow and hail to philanthropists who 'come down handsomely;' he compares the fog to unlimited beer. Scrooge is not really inhuman at the beginning any more than he is at the end. There is a heartiness in his inhospitable sentiments that is akin to humour and therefore to humanity; he is only a crusty old bachelor, and had (I strongly suspect) given away turkeys secretly all his life. The beauty and the real blessing of the story do not lie in the mechanical plot of it, the repentance of Scrooge, probable or improbable; they lie in the great furnace of real happiness that glows through Scrooge and everything around him; that great furnace, the heart of Dickens. Whether the Christmas visions would or would not convert Scrooge, they convert us. Whether or no the visions were evoked by real Spirits of the Past, Present, and Future, they were evoked by that truly exalted order of angels who are correctly called High Spirits. They are impelled and sustained by a quality which our contemporary artists ignore or almost deny, but which in a life decently lived is as normal and attainable as sleep: positive, passionate, conscious joy. The story sings from end to end like a happy man going home; and, like a happy and good man, when it cannot sing it yells. It is lyric and exclamatory, from the first exclamatory words of it. It is strictly *A Christmas Carol*."

In the final analysis, the *Carol* is best read as allegory, and the pre-redemption Scrooge as a symbol of Victorian habits and institutions which were, so far as Dickens could see, nothing short of brutal when it came to the treatment of the poor. George Orwell spoke approvingly of Dickens as "a subversive writer, a radical, one might truthfully say a rebel. Everyone who has read widely in his work has felt this. [George] Gissing, for instance, the best of the writers on Dickens, was anything but a radical himself, and he disapproved of this strain in Dickens and wished it were not there, but it never occurred to him to deny it. In *Oliver Twist, Hard Times, Bleak House, Little Dorrit*, Dickens attacked English institutions with a ferocity that has never been approached."

In its quaint way, the *Carol* was equally subversive.

Phantoms trying in vain to help those less fortunate, depicted by John Leech in a wood engraving for the first edition.

Scrooge and Marley depicted by John Leech in a wood engraving for the first edition.

II

Writing the *Carol*

At New York City's Morgan Library, the staff make a Yuletide ritual of placing Dickens's original *Carol* manuscript on display in the institution's main lobby. Over the course of a month, thousands reverentially file past. "My own and only MS of the Book" Dickens noted on the manuscript's title page. Soon after the book appeared in print, Dickens made a gift of the manuscript to his friend and sometime solicitor Thomas Mitton, who had lent money to the cash-strapped Dickens in early December of 1843, just as the author labored to finish the work. The manuscript thereafter was sold and resold until Pierpont Morgan finally acquired the treasure during the last decade of the 19th century. It has since remained with the rest of Morgan's collection at East 36th Street and Madison Avenue, along with the manuscripts for two other Dickens Christmas books: *The Cricket on the Hearth* and *The Battle of Life.*

The manuscript reveals an author working feverishly on a text that was - nearly miraculously - at once the first and final draft of a masterpiece. Through a maze of x-outs, emendations and cuts and splices, the work as we know it emerges from the frantically-penned page. (Dickens's sister-in-law would, years after the fact, remember how he "wept, and laughed, and wept again, and excited himself in a most extraordinary manner, in the composition, ... thinking whereof, he walked about the black streets of London, fifteen or twenty miles, many a night." Dickens's close friend and authorized biographer John Forster recalled what "a strange mastery seized him" in his work on the *Carol*.) As Paul Davis writes in *The Lives and Times of Ebenezer Scrooge*: "The intensity of his concentration on the tale, written in little more than a month suggests that the little book liberated important areas of his imagination." The words flowed as if the result of Revelation.

Charles Dickens, age 31, began writing *A Christmas Carol* in October of 1843. At that time, his new novel *Martin Chuzzlewit*, which his publishers Chapman & Hall had been issuing as a monthly serial and which Dickens continued to labor on, was proving unpopular with readers - so much so that the publishers threatened to cut his monthly annuity by a (then-substantial) fifty pounds if sales did not improve soon, either with *Chuzzlewit* or something else. The *Carol* proved the answer to this dilemma.

In the end, however, the *Carol* seems not only to have been financially liberating for Dickens, but spiritually liberating as well, after what he himself called the "agonies" of *Chuzzlewit*.

"A study of murderous greed and hypocrisy, [*Chuzzlewit*] called forth less of Dickens's idealism than any of the earlier works," writes Davis. "*Chuzzlewit*'s Dostoyevskian subject matter inverts the Christian virtues. Its worldly characters have faith only in money and hope only for gain, while Charity Pecksniff, the shrewish daughter of its hypocritical villain, performs a perverse denial of her name. The *Carol*, a story of genuine charity, provided welcome relief for both Dickens and his readers from the depressing world of *Martin Chuzzlewit*."

"To keep *Chuzzlewit* going, and do this little book, the *Carol*, in the odd times between parts of it, was, as you may suppose, pretty tight work," Dickens wrote a friend. "When it was done, I broke out like a Madman. ... Such dinings, such dancing, such conjurings, such blind-man's bluffings, such theater-goings, such kissings-out of old years and kissings-in of new ones never took place in these parts before."

*

In his first great literary success - *The Posthumous Papers of the Pickwick Club* (1837) - Dickens had depicted archaic and largely-forgotten Christmas celebrations as once practiced in the great halls of Britain's rural districts. His tale was vibrant and joyful, but it was also nostalgic and elegiac. "In the British imagination," writes Davis, "Christmas was associated with the manor house, peasant revels, and baronial feasts. During the first half of the nineteenth century - particularly in the two decades that preceded the publication of the *Carol* - the growth of industry and cities threatened this rural holiday by threatening its country seat." (The Holiday was also, in later years, viewed skeptically by puritanical Calvinists, who believed it somehow Pagan and unholy, and did not generally believe in "celebrations" of any kind, particularly secular celebrations of religious holidays.)

"Whether lost on the exodus into the new towns or stifled by the smothering hand of Calvinism, the old English

Christmas was largely memory by the beginning of the nineteenth century," Davis continues. "The twelve days (or longer) of Christmas festivity ... celebrated with manorial feasts, yule logs, and feudal games, had disappeared. Sir Walter Scott's loving description of such a Christmas in the introduction to the sixth canto of *Marmion* (1808) is a nostalgic lament in the past tense for the rites of the Christmas feast. ... Washington Irving's benign account of Christmas at Bracebridge Hall (1820), probably the most loving description of a 'merrie English' Christmas ever written, repeatedly reminds the reader that Bracebridge is a 'bigoted devotee of the old school' and his elaborate manorial festivities are 'lingering ... holiday customs and rural games of former times' no longer continued 'in these unceremonious days.' Although [Irving's account] purports to describe the narrator's experiences in nineteenth-century England, its nostalgic tone leads the reader to believe that the sketches actually describe an England of memory that has cast 'a delightful spell over [the narrator's] imagination.' They are remembrances of things past."

Still, at the time Dickens composed the *Carol,* Christmas was ever so slowly beginning to enjoy a revival. Queen Victoria's consort, the German Prince Albert, brought the trappings and traditions of his homeland -

where Christmas remained a cause for strident celebration - to Windsor Castle, where the first British Christmas tree appeared in 1841. (Albert also sent decorated Christmas trees to schools in Windsor and to the local army barracks.) The Royal Family carried the tree into Windsor themselves, decorated it themselves, exchanged gifts, and enjoyed a home-cooked Christmas feast. Press accounts of their family celebration encouraged others to act in imitation, no matter on how small the scale. The first commercially-printed Christmas card made its appearance three years after publication of the *Carol.*

As for Dickens himself, his portrait of a modest Christmas as observed by working poor (such as the Cratchit family) in modern cities - merry and jovial, even if lean when it came to a feast or gifts - probably came in large measure from his own childhood experiences. "The Cratchit family live in a small terraced house which is clearly an evocation of that house in Bayham Street where the Dickens family had moved after their arrival in London," notes Dickens biographer Peter Ackroyd, "and their crippled infant had first been christened not Tiny Tim but 'Tiny Fred' - the name of [Dickens's] own brother who was two years old at the time of their journey to the capital. Some of [Dickens's] earliest memories are here fused

16

together, creating such an entirely new shape that it is perhaps pointless to look for the various scattered 'sources' of which *A Christmas Carol* is made up. It is enough to say that much of its power derives from the buried recollections which animate it."

Dickens's n'er-do-well but nevertheless kind father, John Dickens (model for Wilkins Micawber in *David Copperfield*), had spent much of his childhood at Crewe Hall - a Jacobean mansion located near Crewe Green, east of Crewe, in Cheshire, England - where his father had been butler and where his mother, Charles Dickens's grandmother, worked in service as a housekeeper for many years long after her husband's death. Crewe Hall would have been an outpost where the traditional British Christmas was still observed during the time of John Dickens's youth. Thus he is likely to have carried forth some sense of that tradition within his own family. At least this was probably the case during Charles's very earliest years, before the father's financial recklessness resulted in the Dickens family's economic status being revised from poor to hopeless.

"There is no reason to doubt," writes Ackroyd, "that the Dickens family took Christmas more seriously than many of their contemporaries. John Dickens would have experienced that festival in the opulent setting of Crewe Hall, and there is every reason to suppose that he would try to recreate such an atmosphere in his own home with conjurings, dances, recitations, charades, forfeits, blind-man's-bluffs, and card games like Pope Joan or Speculation."

*

Dickens presaged Scrooge with a key character in *Pickwick*. "In that novel Dickens has Mr. Wardle tell the party that it is customary for everyone to while away the time until midnight, when Christmas is ushered in, by playing games of forfeits or telling ghost stories," writes Dickens scholar Richard Kelly. "Mr. Wardle then relates the tale of a morose, lonely, and mean-spirited sexton named Gabriel Grub who, after being visited by a frightening group of goblins who show him the past and future, is transformed into an amiable man 'who saw that men like himself, who snarled at the mirth and cheerfulness of others, were the foulest weeds on the fair surface of the earth.' Unlike Scrooge, whose conversion is seen and welcomed by all around him, Gabriel could not bear the thought of returning to a place where his repentance would be scoffed at and his reformation disbelieved. He vanishes for ten years and returns 'a ragged, contented, rheumatic old man.'"

In his commentary published with the Yale University Press/Morgan Library facsimile reprint of Dickens's manuscript for *A Christmas Carol,* John Mortimer elaborates: "[Dickens] had written a preliminary sketch for *A Christmas Carol* in *The Pickwick Papers.* There old Wardle, sitting at the fireside of Dingley Dell, tells the story of Gabriel Grubb, a misanthropic sexton, who punished a boy for singing a Christmas Carol by hitting [the child] on the head with his lantern. Grubb, working by night in a churchyard, is then visited by goblins, like the spirits in *A Christmas Carol,* who show him the hardships of the poor."

Scrooge, like Grub, is shown the hardships of the poor, but he is also shown their everlasting perseverance and goodwill, and their understanding and celebration of the Christmas spirit despite strained circumstances. Additionally - and, for Mortimer, perhaps most importantly - Scrooge (unlike Grub) is reminded of the joys of youth. "There's no doubt," writes Mortimer, "... that Dickens saw [Christmas] as a festival for children. 'Happy, happy Christmas,' he wrote in *Pickwick,* 'that can win us back to the delusions of our childhood days.' ... The trouble with Ebenezer Scrooge, the Christmas-hating miser, is that he has completely lost touch with the child within him. The same can be said of all the characters Dickens hates most. His best-loved characters retain their childhood. The members of the Pickwick Club can hardly resist playing leapfrog; Bob Cratchit, Scrooge's underpaid clerk and father of Tiny Tim, goes sliding on the ice in a London street."

George Orwell commented: "No one, at any rate no English writer, has written better about childhood than Dickens. In spite of all the knowledge that has accumulated since, in spite of the fact that children are now comparatively sanely treated, no novelist has shown the same power of entering into the child's point of view. I must have been about nine years old when I first read *David Copperfield*. The mental atmosphere of the opening chapters was so immediately intelligible to me that I vaguely imagined they had been written by a child." But he adds: "A sympathetic attitude towards children was a much rarer thing in Dickens's day than it is now. The early nineteenth century was not a good time to be a child. In Dickens's youth children were still being 'solemnly tried at a criminal bar, where they were held up to be seen', and it was not so long since boys of thirteen had been hanged for petty theft."

There's no doubt that children, especially the children of the poor, dominated the best and most compassionate instincts in Dickens's mind and writing. ("How wise Dickens was," historian Howard Zinn notes "to make readers feel poverty and cruelty through the fate of children who had not reached the age where the righteous and comfortable classes could accuse them of being responsible for their own misery.") Oliver Twist, Nicholas Nickleby, and David Copperfield are the most famous of Dickens's child characters to suffer the severe blows of Victorian poverty, but there were many others as well.

In one of the *Carol's* greatest and most important scenes, Dickens uses children as the ultimate symbols of all that is evil in the dark heart of the British social structure. The Ghost of Christmas Present brings forth "from the foldings of its robe ... two children: wretched, abject, frightful, hideous, miserable." They cling, terrified, to the outside of the ghost's garment. "They were a boy and girl. Yellow meagre, ragged, scowling, wolfish; but prostrate, too, in their humility. Where graceful youth should have filled their features out, and touched them with its freshest tints, a stale and shriveled hand, like that of age, had pinched, and twisted them, and pulled them into shreds. Where angels might have sat enthroned, devils lurked, and glared out menacing. No change, no degradation, no perversion of humanity, in any grade, through all the mysteries of wonderful creation, has monsters half so horrible and dread." When Scrooge asks if the children are those of the Ghost, the latter answers: "They are Man's ... and they cling to me, appealing from their fathers. This boy is Ignorance. This girl is Want. Beware them both, and all of their degree, but most of all beware this boy, for on his brow I see that written which is Doom, unless the writing be erased."

And erase it Dickens certainly wished to do.

III
The *Carol* as Social Commentary

"Dickens's tale of greed and redemption is a heart-warming tale of a Christmas miracle. But there is a dead serious purpose here," writes J.B. Hare. "Dickens takes the mantle of an Old Testament prophet, issuing a stern warning to the capitalist class that they needed to mend their ways, or things would get a lot worse."

"Are there no prisons?" Scrooge asks the two charitable men who dare to visit his office on Christmas Eve, soliciting funds to make "some slight provision for the poor and destitute, who suffer greatly at the present time." After their sad, affirmative response he continues: "And the Union workhouses. Are they still in operation? ... [and] the Treadmill and the Poor Law ... in full vigor?" Again the gentlemen sadly respond *yes*. "Oh," Scrooge answers, "I was afraid from what you said at first, that something had occurred to stop them in their useful courses. I'm very glad to hear it."

As suggested by Scrooge's questions, mid-19th century England was a place of accepted, legislated, legitimized institutional harshness in the treatment of the poor. Governmental response to the needs and problems of the underclass were by turns either nonexistent or sadistic. In the decade prior to his *Carol*, Dickens had exhausted himself writing myriad articles and editorials denouncing the New Poor Law [of 1834], which dramatically cut services and funds for the "idle" poor, encouraged the building of workhouses, tore families apart by demanding that sexes be separated in workhouses, cut workhouse food rations, and in other ways pushed against the general interests of those who needed help the most. (Dickens wrote *Oliver Twist* [1838] as a direct response to the New Poor Law. Thus Oliver's cruel time in the workhouse, and his plaintive, doomed request at dinner: "Please, sir, I want some more.")

Dickens clipped articles from the newspapers concerning a multitude of sanctioned abuses, and made notes - so important to him were the worsening conditions of the nation's outcasts. Ackroyd reports how Dickens read in *The Times* "the accounts of the trial of a young woman who, in her terror of the workhouse, had thrown herself with her baby into the Thames; the child had slipped away from the mother's arms, and drowned, and the rescued mother was found guilty of murder and condemned to death. And Dickens had read, too, of the activities of a certain Sir Peter Laurie, magistrate, who had made it his business to 'put down' the crime of suicide by sentencing to the treadmill any wretches who tried but failed to kill themselves." (In his second Christmas book, *The Chimes* [1844], Dickens would satirize Laurie as "Alderman Cute," and sternly criticize his cruel crusade.)

Where government did little that was productive or positive, private charity tried to do a bit more.

"Charity and charitable enterprises were at the very heart of Victorian life and constituted the main way in which those unable to take care of themselves were taken care of by society," Jane Smiley has written in her short biography of Dickens. "Very few social services as we know them were provided by the government - rather, churches and privately supported charitable institutions, upholding a wide variety of theories and methods, provided education, sustenance, sometimes employment, and care for those in need. Dickens did not uniformly support all of these institutions, especially not those sponsored by Evangelical groups. The combination of puritanical narrowness and

crabbed strictness opposed Dickens's instinctive sense that
true charity was an outgrowth of kindly benevolence and
good cheer. He had his own theories about the failures of
his society and their proper alleviation and he was
frequently in sympathy with radical political ideas. At the
same time, he deeply distrusted social unrest, including
incipient revolutionary movements, labor strikes, or any
potential violent confrontation between classes. Social order
was his highest goal, a social order that recognized the
responsibility of all to all and made plenty of room for the
pleasures of life - entertainment, good fellowship, good food
and drink, congenial surroundings, familial affection. While
he feared social unrest, he deplored any means by which the
moneyed classes might shirk their social responsibilities:
harsh poor laws, legal obfuscation, bureaucratic
incompetence and red tape, failure to attend to public
works and public sanitation, or simple personal selfishness
and profligacy. It can be fairly argued, in this context, that
Dickens never shirked his. His mode of life demonstrated
that he lived by play as well as work, believed equally in the
value of each, and promoted the value of both for all
members of Victorian society."

If Dickens's primary vocation was writer, his second was
most certainly social activist. The author not only preached

reform, but rigorously practiced what he preached. Dickens routinely gave readings and otherwise helped organize fund-raisers for worthy causes of all types - every one of them designed to ameliorate and improve the conditions of the poor. Most notably, he worked in partnership with Angela Burdett-Coutts, heiress to the Coutts banking fortune, on numerous charitable projects including the Urania Cottage to help retrain and rehabilitate unwed mothers and former prostitutes.

*

"The conditions of the [*Carol's*] creation can be located firmly within [a certain] context," notes Alex Ogg. "*A Christmas Carol* was directly inspired by the October [1843] publication of *The Second Report (Trades & Manufactures) of the Children's Employment Commission*, with its first-hand testimony of the conditions endured by young labor. Dickens had spoken in Manchester that same month and been appalled by the squalor of workers in the world's first industrialized city. He thereafter resolved to write a ghost story for Christmas that would prick the consciences of the moneyed classes who had so materialistically benefited from industrialization."

What Dickens said in his speech to the first annual meeting of the Manchester Athenaeum - an institution recently founded with the mission to bring literacy and culture to "laboring classes" - was this: "Thousands of immortal creatures are condemned ... to tread, not what our great poet calls the 'primrose path to the everlasting bonfire' but over jagged flints and stones laid down by brutal ignorance." Ignorance, he told his listeners, was "the most prolific parent of misery and crime." Not much later, in an *Examiner* editorial, he wrote: "Side by side with Crime, Disease, and Misery in England, Ignorance is always brooding, and is always certain to be found."

Round about this same time, Dickens also visited Samuel Starey's "Ragged School" - an earnest effort to provide rudimentary educations to children of the London slums, this particular school being located on Field Lane in the rancid neighborhood of Saffron Hill. Writing to Angela Burdett-Coutts with a recommendation that she donate to the Ragged School, he described the Saffron Hill district as defined by "a sickening atmosphere, in the midst of taint and dirt and pestilence; with all the deadly sins let loose, howling and shrieking at the doors. ... I have very seldom seen, in all the strange and dreadful things I have seen in London and elsewhere, anything so shocking as the dire neglect of soul and body exhibited in [the homeless children of Saffron Hill]." These children routinely got what they needed for survival through either thieving or prostitution. "Many of them retire for the night, if they retire at all, under the dry arches of bridges and viaducts; under porticoes, sheds and carts; to outhouses; in sawpits; on staircases." (In the novel *Oliver Twist*, Dickens located Fagin's Den squarely within the heart of Saffron Hill.)

Poverty - especially childhood poverty - was something to which Dickens could relate quite personally. Dickens's own childhood had been shaped and defined by abject want. As a hungry and neglected wretch of a boy, the ten year old Dickens had spent long days working in a putrid London warehouse which lay decrepit above the Thames at 30 Hungerford Stairs, pasting labels on pots of blacking. "The task was monotonous, interminable," wrote critic Ben Ray Redman in the 1930s. "The filth and litter of decay surrounded him, and from the cellars of the building rose the constant squeaking and scrabbling of great gray rats. At night when his work was finished he would go home to a miserable lodging where he supped on bread and cheese. And every Sunday without fail he spent within the gloomy confines of the Marshalsea prison where, according to the quaint custom of the time, his father, who had been committed for debt, was living with his wife [and] several [smaller] children ..."

Dickens declared of that time in his life: "No words can express the secret agony of my soul. The deep remembrance of the sense I had of being utterly neglected and hopeless; of the shame I felt in my position; of the misery that it was to my young heart to believe that, day by day, what I had learned and thought, and delighted in, and raised my fancy and my emulation up by, was passing away from me, never to be brought back any more; cannot be written."

So many years after this nightmare, inspired by the *The Second Report* and his own haunted memories, Dickens briefly dabbled with the idea of writing a pamphlet titled *An Appeal to the People of England on behalf of the Poor Man's Child.* But he soon abandoned this in favor of something else, something better which - he promised a friend - would deal a "literary sledgehammer blow" for the same cause. Dickens's sledgehammer proved to be the *Carol* - the "little scheme," as he described it to an associate, upon which he began work immediately upon his return to London from Manchester.

The great Dickens biographer Edgar Johnson has commented that in *A Christmas Carol* "Dickens makes of the Christmas spirit a symbolic criticism of the relations that throughout almost all the rest of the year subsist between men and their fellow men. It is a touchstone revealing and drawing forth the gold of generosity ordinarily crusted over with selfish habit, an earnest of the truth that our natures are not entirely and essentially devoted to competitive struggle. Dickens is certain that the enjoyment most men are able to feel in the happiness of others can play a larger part than it does in the tenor of their lives. The sense of brotherhood, he feels, can be broadened to a deeper and more active concern for the welfare of all mankind. It is in this light that Dickens sees the spirit of Christmas. ... The triumphal meaning of Christmas peals in those angel voices ringing through the sky: 'On earth peace, good will toward men.' It is a sign and an affirmation that men do not live by bread alone, that they do not live for barter and sale alone. ... England's prosperity was not so uncertain - if, indeed, any nation's ever is - that she needed to be parsimonious and cruel to her waifs and strays, or even to the incompetents and casualties of life. To neglect the poor, to deny them education, to give them no protection from covetous employers, to let them be thrown out of work and fall ill and die in filthy surroundings that then engender spreading pestilence, to allow them to be harried by misery into crime - all these turned out in the long run to be the most disastrous shortsightedness. That is what the Ghost of Christmas Present means in showing Scrooge the two ragged and wolfish children glaring beneath his robes."

Ignorance and Want depicted by John Leech in a wood engraving for the first edition.

IV

Dickens's Later Christmas Books

Following the success of the *Carol,* Dickens continued for several years to churn out novella-length Christmas tales for his ready-market of readers. These were *The Chimes: A Goblin Story of Some Bells that Rang an Old Year Out and a New Year In* (1844), *The Cricket on the Hearth* (1845), *The Battle of Life* (1846), and *The Haunted Man and the Ghost's Bargain* (1848). Dickens did not write a Christmas book for 1847, and discontinued them altogether after 1848. Subsequently, as the editor and publisher of the weekly magazines *Household Words* (1850-1858) and *All the Year Round* (1859-1867), he published a number of additional, shorter Christmas tales of relatively minor importance.

Dickens wrote *The Chimes* while on an extended stay in Genoa, Italy. The story focuses on Toby (aka, *Trotty*) Veck, an impoverished ticket porter whose perspective is changed from one of despair to one of hope and optimism by the spirits of the chimes on New Year's Eve.

John Forster notes that Dickens gathered the germ of the idea for the novel one day when he heard the clamor of Genoese church bells peeling not far from his rented villa. "All Genoa lay beneath him," writes Forster, "and up from it, with some sudden set of the wind, came in one fell sound the clang and clash of all its steeples, pouring into his ears, again and again, in a tuneless, grating, discordant, jerking, hideous vibration that made his ideas 'spin round and round till they lost themselves in a whirl of vexation and giddiness, and dropped down dead.'"

Forster identifies Dickens's intentions here, as in the *Carol*, as striking "a blow for the poor. They had always been his clients, they had never been forgotten in any of his books, but here nothing else was to be remembered ... he had come to have as little faith for the putting down of any serious evil, as in a then notorious city alderman's gabble for the putting down of suicide. The latter had stirred his indignation to its depths just before he came to Italy, and his increased opportunities of solitary reflection since had strengthened and extended it. When he came therefore to think of his new story for Christmas time, he resolved to make it a plea for the poor ... He was to try and convert Society, as he had converted Scrooge, by showing that its happiness rested on the same foundations as those of the individual, which are mercy and charity not less than justice."

In general, *The Chimes* adopts a far more didactic and emphatic tone than the *Carol* in castigating those who do not possess or display sympathy for their less fortunate brethren. "Who turns his back upon the fallen and disfigured of his kind," Dickens wrote, "abandons them as vile; and does not trace and track with pitying eyes the unfenced precipice by which they fell from good - grasping in their fall some tufts and shreds of that lost soil, and clinging to them still when bruised and dying in the gulf below; does wrong to Heaven and man, to time and to eternity."

"*The Chimes*," writes Chesterton, "is, like the *Carol*, an appeal for charity and mirth, but it is a stern and fighting appeal: if the [previous Christmas book was a] carol, [*The Chimes*] is a Christmas war-song. In it Dickens hurled himself with even more than his usual militant joy and scorn into an attack upon a cant, which he said made his blood boil. This cant was nothing more nor less than the whole tone taken by three-quarters of the political and economic world towards the poor. It was a vague and vulgar Benthamism with a rollicking Tory touch in it. It explained to the poor their duties with a cold and coarse philanthropy unendurable by any free man. It had also at its command a kind of brutal banter, a loud good humor which Dickens sketches savagely in Alderman Cute. He fell furiously on all their ideas: the cheap advice to live cheaply, the base advice to live basely, above all, the preposterous primary assumption that the rich are to advise the poor and not the poor the rich. There were and are hundreds of these benevolent bullies. Some say that the poor should give up having children, which means that they should give up their great virtue of sexual sanity. Some say that they should give up 'treating' each other, which means that they should give up all that remains to them of the virtue of hospitality. Against all of this Dickens thundered very thoroughly in *The Chimes.*"

Chesterton continues: "The moral of this matter in *The Chimes* is essential. Dickens had sympathy with the poor in the Greek and literal sense; he suffered with them mentally; for the things that irritated them were the things that irritated him. He did not pity the people, or even champion the people, or even merely love the people; in this matter he was the people. He alone in our literature is the voice not merely of the social substratum, but even of the subconsciousness of the substratum. He utters the secret anger of the humble. He says what the uneducated only think, or even only feel, about the educated. And in nothing is he so genuinely such a voice as in this fact of his fiercest mood being reserved for methods that are counted scientific and progressive. ... Of all this anger, good or bad, Dickens is the voice of an accusing energy. When, in *A Christmas Carol*, Scrooge refers to the surplus population, the Spirit tells him, very justly, not to speak till he knows what the surplus is and where it is. The implication is severe but sound. When a group of superciliously benevolent economists look down into the abyss for the surplus population, assuredly there is only one answer that should be given to them; and that is to say, 'If there is a surplus, you are a surplus.'"

Most importantly, Chesterton points out, "Dickens was at one with the poor in [the] chief matter of Christmas, in the matter, that is, of special festivity. There is nothing on which the poor are more criticized than on the point of spending large sums on small feasts; and though there are material difficulties, there is nothing in which they are more right. It is said that a Boston paradox-monger said, 'Give us the luxuries of life and we will dispense with the necessities.' But it is the whole human race that says it, from the first savage wearing feathers instead of clothes to the last costermonger having a treat instead of three meals."

*

Dickens's third Christmas book, *The Cricket on the Hearth*, tells the tale of John and Dot Peerybingle whose marriage is threatened by the wide difference in their ages and John's suspicions of Dot's infidelity. Seeking solace and guidance, John enters into commerce with the spirit of the cricket on the hearth, whose chirping is said to bring luck. Understandings are reached, and marital peace restored in counterpoint with a side-story: that of the bitter and cold-hearted toymaker Tackleton experiencing a Scrooge-like redemption.

Chesterton thought Dickens's *Cricket* a minor effort. "The tale itself," he wrote, " ... is a little too comfortable to be quite convincing. *A Christmas Carol* is the conversion of an anti-Christmas character. *The Chimes* is a slaughter of anti-Christmas characters. *The Cricket*, perhaps, fails for lack of this crusading note. For everything has its weak side, and when full justice has been done to this neglected note of poetic comfort, we must remember that it has its very real weak side. The defect of it in the work of Dickens was that he tended sometimes to pile up the cushions until none of the characters could move. He is so much interested in effecting his state of static happiness that he forgets to make a story at all. His princes at the start of the story begin to live happily ever afterwards. ... He makes his characters so comfortable that his characters begin to dream and drivel. And he makes his reader so comfortable that his reader goes to sleep."

*

Unlike Dickens's previous Christmas stories, *The Battle of Life* operated without the aid of ghosts, goblins or any other supernatural element. In this eminently human story, the daughters of the cynical Doctor Jeddler demonstrate their love through sacrifices which change Jeddler's jaded view of life. The tone is melodrama, and the work - virtually all scholars agree - painfully insufficient. Contemporary critics came away feeling this story was grossly underdeveloped, shabby and offhand. *The Times* called it "intrinsically puerile and stupid ... a twaddling manifestation of silliness, [and] simply ridiculous." The paper went on to blame Dickens for "the deluge of trash" then constituting the Christmas book publishing phenomenon (all of it inspired by the success of Dickens's offerings), and called *The Battle of Life* "the very worst" of the lot, without "one spark of originality, of truth, of probability, of nature, of beauty." *The Morning Chronicle* described the book as a package of "exaggerated, absurd, impossible sentimentality." Nevertheless, the volume sold 23,000 copies on the day of publication.

The book had evidently been a hard one for him to write. "I cancelled the beginning of a first scene - which I have never done before - and, with a notion in my head, ran wildly about and about it, and could not get the idea into any natural socket," he wrote a friend from Switzerland, where he was staying that September and October of 1846, while also at work on *Dombey and Son*. A week or so into the Christmas project, he considered consigning the whole tale to the dustbin. "I fear there may be NO CHRISTMAS BOOK. If I had nothing but the Christmas book to do, I WOULD do it; but I get horrified and distressed beyond conception at the prospect of being jaded when I come to the other ... I am sick, giddy, and capriciously despondent. I have bad nights; am full of disquietude and anxiety; and am constantly haunted by the idea that I am wasting the marrow of the larger book, and ought to be at rest." Even as he approached the end of the story, he still seemed unsettled by it. During the last week of the composition, he repeatedly dreamed that it was "a series of chambers impossible to be got to rights or got out of, through which I wandered drearily all night."

Thackeray summed up *The Battle of Life* as "a wretched affair." In later years, Dickens confessed that he thought the story should never have been written.

*

When crafting his final Christmas book - *The Haunted Man and the Ghost's Bargain* - the author once again relied on aid from the spirit world. Here we have Mr. Redlaw - a chemistry professor tormented by bitter memories. Redlaw is visited on Christmas Eve by a phantom, a doppelganger of himself, who bestows the gift of forgetting all painful slices of the past. As part of the phantom's spell, it is also the case that those who henceforth come into contact with the professor will as well lose their own remembrances of past losses and sadnesses. This "gift" spawns Faustian results that are eventually only reversed through the inherent goodness of a naïve and selfless woman who has known her share of tragedy and possesses more than her share of sad but cherished memories.

Of this tale, Ackroyd comments: "The theme ... revolves around Dickens's belief that memory is a softening and chastening power, that the recollection of old sufferings and old wrongs can be used to touch the heart and elicit sympathy with the sufferings of others. ... For it was his suffering and the memory of his sufferings which had given him the powerful sympathy of the great writer, just as his recollection of those harder days inspired him with that pity for the poor and the dispossessed which was a mark of his social writings." Writing to John Forster, Dickens explained: "Of course, my point is that bad and good are inextricably linked in remembrance, and that you could not choose the enjoyment of recollecting only the good. To have all the best of it you must remember the worst also."

The Haunted Man, writes Edgar Johnson, "is a weak performance. ... Yet, feeble though the tale is, it is significant because it reflects the inward preoccupations with which Dickens was struggling. Like Redlaw, he himself is a famous and outwardly successful man. In the imaginative laboratory of his art, as in Redlaw's test tubes and retorts, there are hosts of spectral shapes like those glass vessels with their chemicals, all subject to his power to uncombine and recombine. But like Redlaw he has known wrongs and sufferings from under the burden of which he cannot escape, until he asks himself whether the years bring anything but 'More figures in the lengthening sum of recollection that we work and work at to our torment ... ' Does he indulge his griefs, ever evoking these phantoms of past and present despondency? It matters not; bidden or unbidden, they come."

Critics hated *The Haunted Man* just as much as they had *The Battle of Life.* An anonymous reviewer writing for *Macphail's Edinburgh Ecclesiastical Journal* echoed the view of most of his brethren when he said: "Let us now have a few more returns of Christmas, and Mr. Dickens will have destroyed his reputation as a tale-writer. We earnestly recommend him to quit the twenty-fifth of December ..."

Despite such sneers, *The Haunted Man* - like every Dickens Christmas book before it - sold briskly: eighteen thousand copies on December 19th, 1848, the first day of publication. Nevertheless, Dickens took the unsolicited advice offered by *Macphail's* and quit the Christmas book trade for good.

Toby (Trotty) Veck of The Chimes *depicted by John Leech in a wood engraving for the first edition.*

V

Dickens and the *Carol* as a Reading Performance

Dickens chose the *Carol* as the text for his first public reading in 1853. He delivered the story in a form carefully edited so as to reduce the spoken-word version to an appropriate length for such a presentation, while at the same time preserving the tone, elegance and message of the piece. Thereafter, the author delivered the tale a total of 127 times until the year of his death, 1870, when it served as the centerpiece for his farewell performance. (Dickens's "prompt" copy of the *Carol*, heavily edited and annotated for use in his readings, today resides in the Berg Collection of the New York Public Library, on Fifth Avenue.)

Dickens had long been enthralled with the stage as a medium and the theater as an endeavor. He co-wrote plays with such partners as Wilkie Collins, allowed dramatizations of his various stories and novels, cultivated friendships among actors (including the great William

Macready) during an era when "proper" people normally did no such thing, and even scheduled special morning readings in order to accommodate members of the acting profession who were themselves professionally engaged in the evenings. He'd once, as a young man, had aspirations to the stage; he considered himself an excellent actor. Thus his readings of the *Carol* (and other works) were more than mere readings; they were dramatic renderings with Dickens adopting the facial characteristics and particular intonations of the range of characters.

From the podium where Dickens stood, Scrooge glared down at audiences and condemned all things merry - his voice a commanding, censorious thing. Bob Cratchit's face lit up with innocent goodwill, as did his manner of speaking. And the Ghost of Christmas Present's booming, benevolent presence filled the hall as nothing else could. Dickens brought them all wonderfully to life on stage, just as he had on paper. "It was more than a reading," notes Johnson, "it was an extraordinary exhibition of acting ... without a single prop or bit of costume, by changes of voice, by gesture, by vocal expression, Dickens peopled his stage with a throng of characters."

The first public readings were given at the Birmingham Town Hall on the dates of December 27th, 29th and 30th, 1853 for the benefit of the Birmingham and Midland Institute - a pioneer endeavor to provide adult scientific and technical education for the working class. "The first night's reading of *A Christmas Carol* on December 27th was attended by two thousand people," notes Johnson, "who listened spellbound for three full hours, and repeatedly burst into tumultuous applause. After an almost equally successful reading of *The Cricket on the Hearth*, on the 29th, he gave a second reading of the *Carol* on the 30th, at reduced prices, before an assemblage of twenty-five hundred working people, for whom Dickens had requested that most of the vast auditorium be reserved. These, he thought, were the best audience of the three. 'They lost nothing, misinterpreted nothing, followed everything closely, laughed and cried ... and animated me to that extent that I felt as if we were all bodily going up into the clouds together.'" Going forward, Dickens was to always insist that a set amount of seats for his readings be set aside for sale at only a shilling a piece, so that working-people (many of them illiterate) might attend and experience his stories.

For five years, all of Dickens's public readings were for charity. After this - while continuing to give many benefit performances - he also toured for his own profit. In the end he delivered a total of 423 readings on both sides of the Atlantic, including in his programs various sections from *David Copperfield, Oliver Twist* and other works.

An American journalist, Kate Field, has left us a vivid account of the experience of watching him read the *Carol.* According to Field, Dickens would start out in a low and almost monotonous rhythm which quickly gained speed as soon as characters began to speak. "Then there comes the change when Scrooge, upon going home, 'saw in the knocker Marley's face!' Of course Scrooge saw it, because the expression of Dickens's face, as he rubs his eyes and stares makes me see it, 'with a dismal light about it, like a bad lobster in a dark cellar.' ... Dickens's expression [in relating Fezziwig's ball] is delightfully comic, while his complete rendering of the dance where 'all were top couples at last, and not a bottom one to help them,' is owning to the inimitable action of his hands. They actually perform upon the table, as if it were the floor of Fezziwig's room, and every finger were a leg belonging to one of the Fezziwig family."

Field continued: "What Dickens does is frequently infinitely better than anything he says, or the way he says it;

48

yet the doing is as delicate and intangible as the odor of violets, and can be no better indicated. Nothing of its kind can be more touchingly beautiful than the manner in which Bob Cratchit - previous to proposing 'a merry Christmas to us all, my dears, God bless us' - stoops down, with tears in his eyes, and places Tiny Tim's withered little hand in his, 'as if he loved the child, and wished to keep him by his side, and dreaded that he might be taken from him.' It is a pantomime worthy of the finest actor."

Dickens gave his very last public reading - which had been advertised as his farewell performance - at London's St. James Hall on March 15th, 1870. The program included *A Christmas Carol* and a popular excerpt - The Trial - from *Pickwick*. Dickens's road manager, George Dolby, remembered him on this final night, a "spare figure ... faultlessly attired in evening dress, the gas-light streaming down upon him, illuminating every feature of his familiar face." Charles (Charley) Dickens Jr. would later comment: "I thought I had never heard him read ... so well and with so little effort."

At the end of the night, recalled to the stage by the seemingly endless applause and cheers of his audience, he spoke his last few public words: "Ladies and Gentlemen, it would be worse than idle - for it would be hypocritical and unfeeling - if I were to disguise that I close this episode in my life with feelings of very considerable pain. ... From these garish lights I vanish now forever more, with a heartfelt, grateful, respectful, and affectionate farewell." As Charley Dickens remembered, these words were followed by a moment of hush, and then "a storm of cheering as I have never seen equaled in my life. ... [My father] was deeply touched that night, but infinitely sad and broken." He would be dead within three months.

*

Dickens and his wife Catherine had ten children: seven boys and three girls, one dying in infancy. The second youngest of the boys, Henry Fielding Dickens, attended Cambridge, became a barrister, judge and Common Serjeant of London, and was knighted in 1922. Sir Henry - who was, by the way, the grandfather of novelist Monica Dickens - made it a Christmas tradition at his home on Mulberry Walk in London to perform a reading of the *Carol* in the style and with the inflections he remembered so well from his father. During these performances he would wear a

50

geranium, his father's favorite flower, and lean on the same velvet-covered reading stand used by Dickens during his reading tours.

Sir Henry had listened to his father many times; older members of his audience said his presentation was amazingly like that given by Dickens himself. To celebrate his eightieth birthday in 1929, Sir Henry reportedly went through the whole of the *Carol* without a hitch, his false teeth loosening and creating an amusing effect: "I know him - Marley's ghosht!" - or so recalled Henry's grandson, Cedric Dickens. From 1914 onward until his death in 1932, Sir Henry regularly performed recitals of the *Carol* and others of his father's works in support such charities as the Red Cross, continuing in his generous father's footsteps.

*Scrooge and Bob Cratchit after Scrooge's conversion, depicted by
John Leech in a wood engraving for the first edition.*

VI

Epilogue

In mid-December 2010, New York's Housing Works Bookstore Café in Soho hosted a marathon reading of *A Christmas Carol.* A large number of the city's best and hippest writers - plus a few actors - took fifteen minute turns at the microphone. "I love Charles Dickens ... " said novelist Mary Gaitskill. "I think people who think he's corny just can't read."

In fine Dickens tradition, *30 Rock's* Scott Adsit dressed up his reading with great voices, accents and facial impressions. Novelist and British transplant Patrick McGrath told a reporter for *The New Yorker* that he found it much easier to read Dickens than to read his own work. "Dickens's rhythms seem made to be read aloud," he said. "Especially when he gets quite soppy - you can be bombastic with it."

Francine Prose got the honor of presenting the famous scene wherein the reformed Scrooge shouts down from his window and orders a turkey: "Not the little prize Turkey: the big one." (Prose announced to the crowd her delight that her part was about food; even better, "about takeout." Prose added: "It's very moving to me. Here are all these people who could be out shopping for useless presents, and they're sitting here, listening to Dickens.")

Appropriately, proceeds went to a worthy cause. Housing Works is a unique and complex institution. It is a bookstore, a café, an event space, and a charity. 100% of profits go to help people with HIV/AIDS. One senses that Dickens would approve.

~ finis ~

Works Cited

Ackroyd, Peter. *Dickens.* 1991.

Chesterton, G.K. *Charles Dickens.* 1906.

Davis, Paul. *The Lives and Times of Ebenezer Scrooge.* 1990.

Dickens, Charles. *A Christmas Carol: A Facsimile Edition of the Autograph Manuscript in the Pierpont Morgan Library.* 1993.

Dickens, Charles. *The Battle of Life.* 1846.

Dickens, Charles. *The Chimes: A Goblin Story of Some Bells that Rang an Old Year Out and a New Year In.* 1844.

Dickens, Charles. *The Cricket on the Hearth.* 1845.

Dickens, Charles. *The Haunted Man and the Ghost's Bargain.* 1848.

Dickens, Charles. *The Posthumous Papers of the Pickwick Club*. 1837.

Dickens, Henry Fielding. *Memories of My Father*. 1928.

Forster, John. *The Life of Charles Dickens*. 1872-74.

Gissing, George. *Charles Dickens: A Critical Study*. 1898.

Irving, Washington. *The Sketch Book of Geoffrey Crayon, Gent*. 1820.

Johnson, Edgar. *Charles Dickens: His Tragedy and Triumph*. 1952.

Minkel, Elizabeth. "A *Christmas Carol* Marathon." *The New Yorker Blog: Book Bench*. December 20th, 2010.

Orwell, George. "Charles Dickens" in *The Collected Essays, Journalism and Letters of George Orwell*. 1968.

Scott, Sir Walter. *Marmion*. 1808.

Smiley, Jane. *Charles Dickens*. 2002.

About the Author

Michael Norris lives and writes in northern California.